Jack Johnson Brushfire Fairytales

Transcribed by Jeff Jacobson and Paul Pappas

Cover photo by J. P. Plunier

Album art direction and design by J. P. Plunier and Mike King

ISBN 1-57560-604-6

Visit our website at www.cherrylane.com

Jack Johnson

Jack Johnson's name first intersected with the music scene when G. Love and Special Sauce chose his composition "Rodeo Clowns" to be the first single from 1999's *Philadelphonic*. "Rodeo Clowns," on which Johnson also performed, made an impressive impact at radio, further raising Johnson's profile...but still only providing the music community with a glimpse of his scope, talent, and story.

Johnson has long been a huge figure in a world parallel to our musical one as a world-renowned surfer. Having practically learned to surf as he learned to walk, you might say that he has grown up on his board. Born and raised in Hawaii, he began surfing the universally revered and feared Pipeline at age 10. By 17, he'd made the finals at the Pipe trials, becoming the youngest invitee ever to do so at the prestigious event.

Despite having scored a pro contract with Quiksilver before he was even out of high school, young Johnson gravitated away from competition in favor of creativity. He left the island for the University of California at Santa Barbara, later graduating with a degree in film. He wasted no time in utilizing his cinematography skills, racking up film credits including *All for One* and *The Show*, as well as the odd music video, before leaving on a summer sabbatical that took him across Europe in a camper van.

Returning to Hawaii, he reunited with old friends Chris Malloy and Emmett Malloy to conceive and create the acclaimed feature *Thicker Than Water*. Hailed as a return to the purist beauty of early surf cinema, *Thicker Than Water* was a landmark for Johnson on two levels: First, it marked his most significant work as a cinematographer to date; second, and perhaps even more importantly, it was during the scoring of the film that Johnson found his musical voice.

Having played guitar for most of his life in a succession of popular if not remarkable outfits, *Thicker Than Water* marked the first time Johnson would step up to the mike as a full-on singer/songwriter. His soulful folk tunes, inflected occasionally with blues and hip-hop flavorings, soon began circulating in all corners of the global surf community, both as legitimate recordings and bootlegs. By the time *Thicker Than Water* was named *Surfer* magazine's Video of the Year and its follow-up, *The September Sessions,* nabbed the Adobe Highlight Awards at the ESPN Film Festival, labels were wining and dining Johnson and friend-and-collaborator-turned-manager, Emmett Malloy.

In keeping with the ethos that guided him away from a pro sports career in favor of a creative existence, Johnson opted to release his debut album, *Brushfire Fairytales,* on Enjoy Records, an upstart indie founded by veteran A&R man Andy Factor and manager/producer J. P. Plunier. Produced by Plunier, *Brushfire Fairytales* is an impressive debut on numerous levels: From the opening "Inaudible Melodies"—which seems to boil Johnson's personal philosophy down to a chorus of "Slow down everyone/You're moving too fast"—to the psychedelic "Bubble Toes," it's a multi-faceted work by a modern-day journeyman.

In the words of *Surfer* magazine: "Athlete, artist, musician, filmmaker...Jack Johnson is a legend. He is one of those people who is real on the first encounter, showing a fine example of a humble and well-mannered human being."

Contents

4   Inaudible Melodies

10   Middle Man

13   Posters

17   Sexy Plexi

20   Flake

28   Bubble Toes

32   Fortunate Fool

36   The News

39   Drink the Water

44   Mudfootball (For Moe Lerner)

47   F-Stop Blues

50   Losing Hope

53   It's All Understood

58   *Guitar Notation Legend*

INAUDIBLE MELODIES

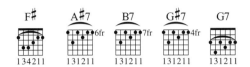

Words and Music by
Jack Johnson

Intro
Slowly ♩ = 76

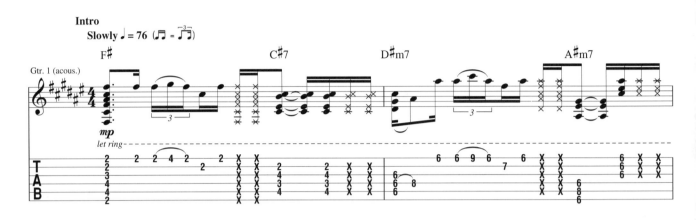

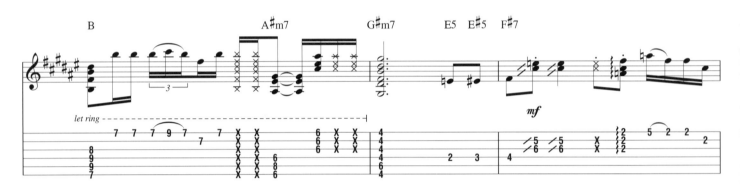

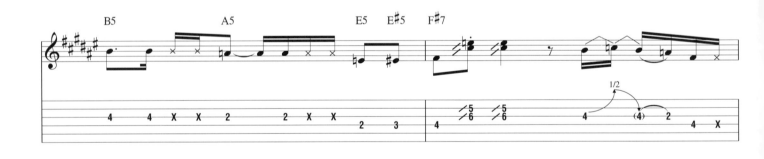

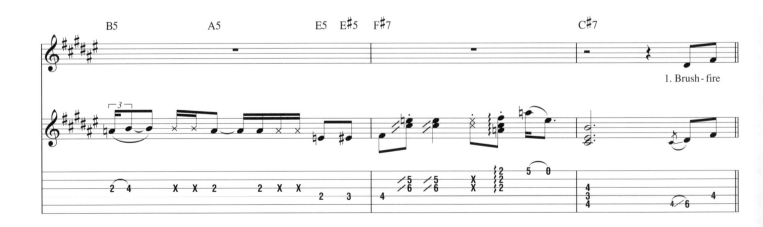

1. Brush-fire

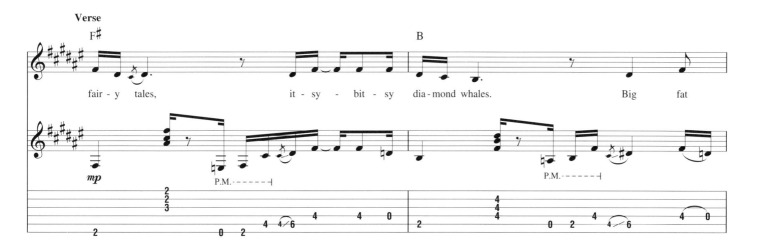

fair-y tales, it-sy - bit-sy dia-mond whales. Big fat

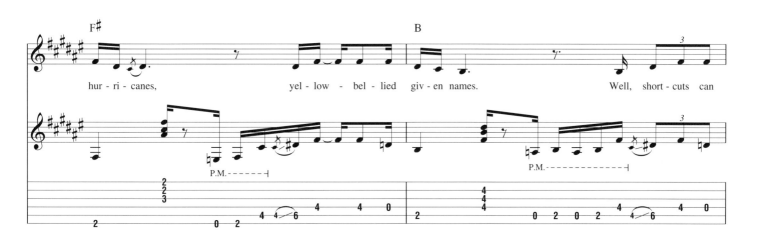

hur-ri - canes, yel-low - bel - lied giv-en names. Well, short - cuts can

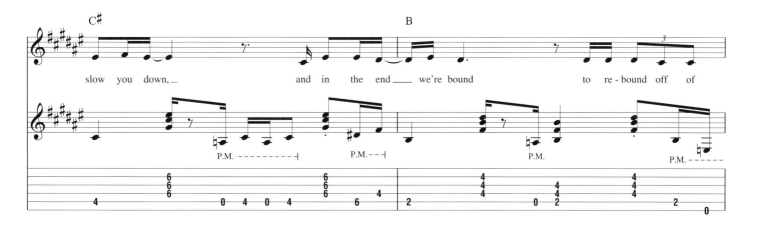

slow you down,__ and in the end __ we're bound to re-bound off of

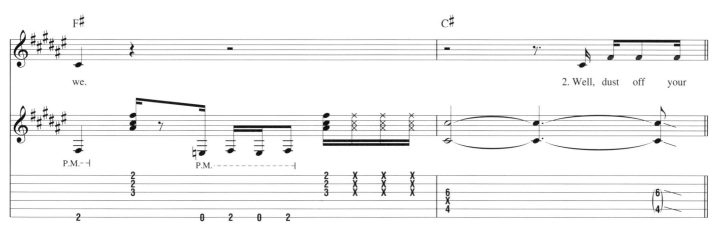

we. 2. Well, dust off your

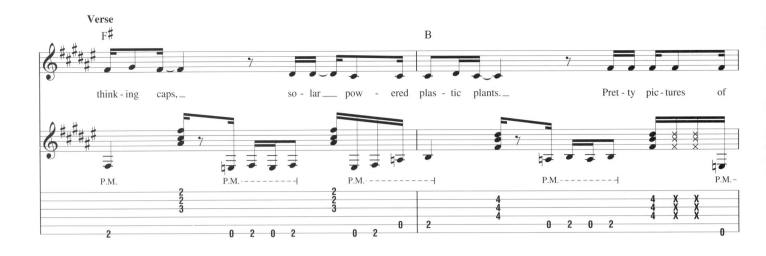

think-ing caps,____ so-lar____ pow-ered plas-tic plants.____ Pret-ty pic-tures of

things we ate,____ we are on-ly what____ we hate. But in the long

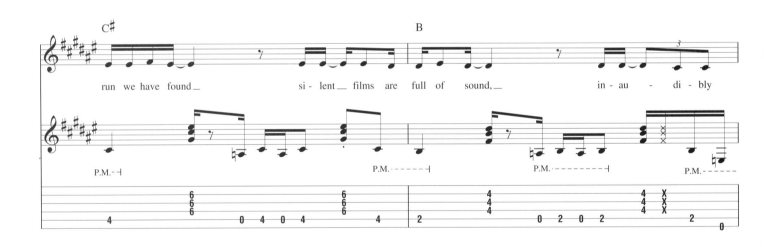

run we have found____ si-lent____ films are full of sound,____ in-au - di-bly

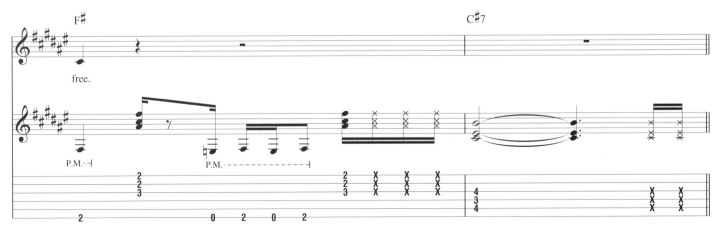

free.

Chorus

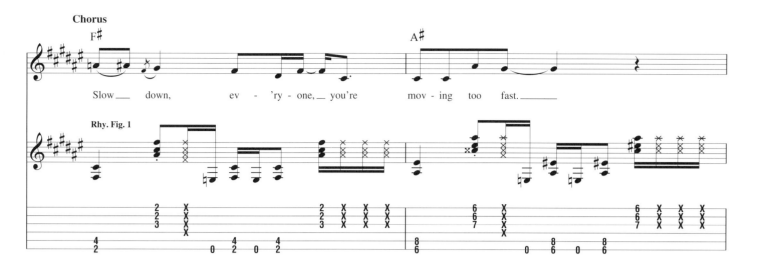

Slow down, ev - 'ry - one, you're mov - ing too fast.

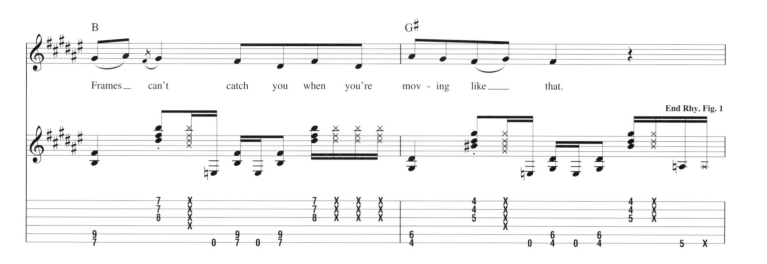

Frames can't catch you when you're mov - ing like that.

Gtr. 1: w/ Rhy. Fig. 1 (1 1/2 times)

In - au - di - ble mel - o - dies serve nar - ra - tion - al strat - e - gies.

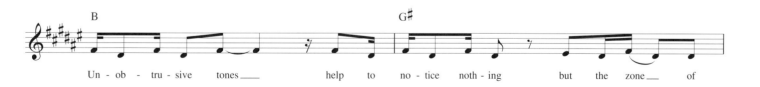

Un - ob - tru - sive tones help to no - tice noth - ing but the zone of

vi - su - al rel - e - van - cy. Frame - lines tell me what to see,

chop - ping like an axe or may - be Eis - en - stein should just re - lax.___

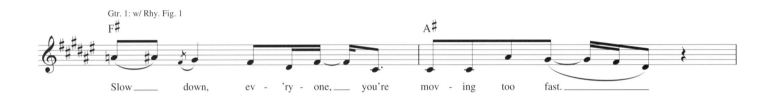

Slow ___ down, ev - 'ry - one, ___ you're mov - ing too fast. _____

Frames ___ can't catch you when you're mov - ing like _____ that.

Guitar Solo

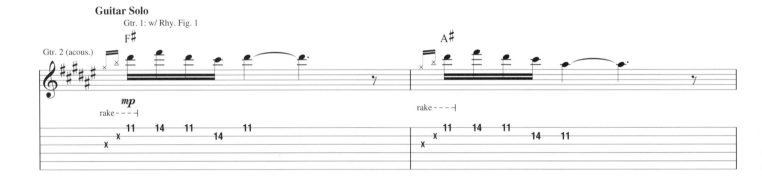

Well,

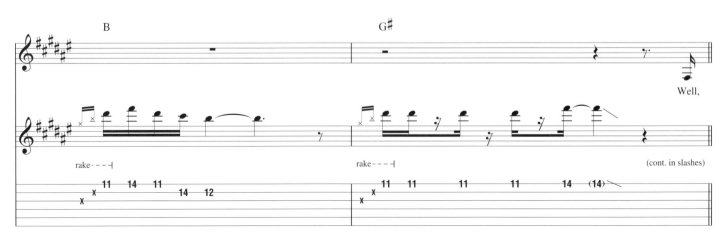

Bridge

Pla - to's cave ___ is full of freaks ___ de - mand - ing re - funds for the things they've seen. ___ I

wish they could ___ be - lieve ___ in all ___ the things ___ that nev - er ___ made the screen. ___ And just

Chorus

Gtr. 1: w/ Rhy. Fig. 1 (2 times)
Gtr. 2 tacet

slow ___ down, ev - 'ry - one, ___ you're mov - ing too fast. ___ Frames ___ can't catch you when you're

mov - ing like ___ that. Slow down, ev - 'ry - one, ___ you're mov - ing too fast. ___

Frames ___ can't catch you when you're mov - ing like ___ that, mov - ing ___ too...

Outro

Gtr. 1

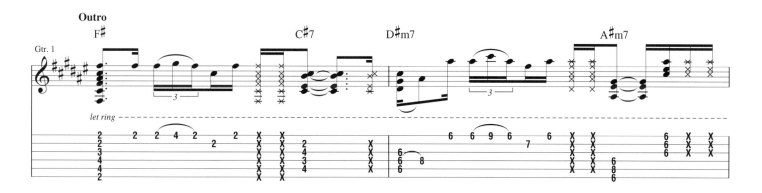

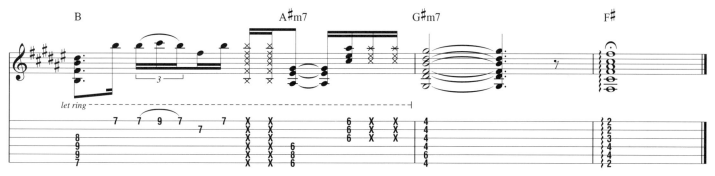

MIDDLE MAN

Words and Music by
Jack Johnson

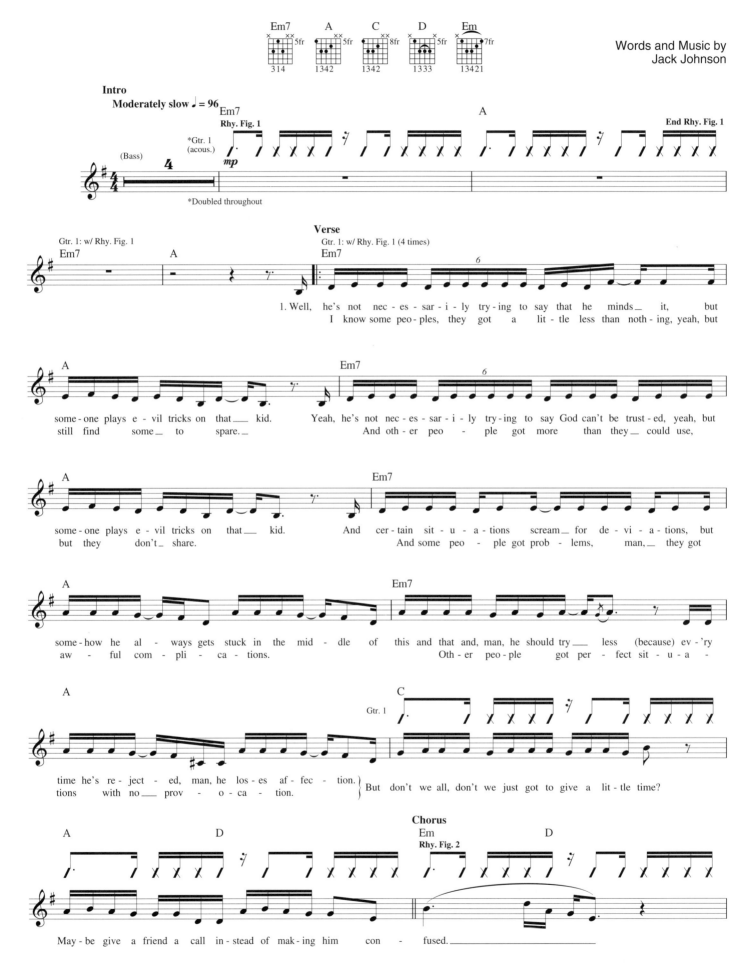

Gtr. 1: w/ Rhy. Fig. 2 (2 times)

What a ter-ri-ble thing___ for you___ to do.___

What an aw-ful thing___ for you___ to say - ee.

1.

What a ter-ri-ble thing___ for you___ to re - lay.___

Gtr. 1
Riff A

*Chord symbols reflect overall harmony.

Gtr. 1 tacet

2.

2. Well, What a ter-ri-ble thing___ for you... Con - fused.___

Gtr. 1: w/ Rhy. Fig. 1 (3 times)

What a ter-ri-ble thing___ for you___ to do.___

What an aw-ful thing___ for you___ to say -

- ee.

What a ter-ri-ble thing___ for you___ to re -

Gtr. 1: w/ Riff A

lay.___

Interlude

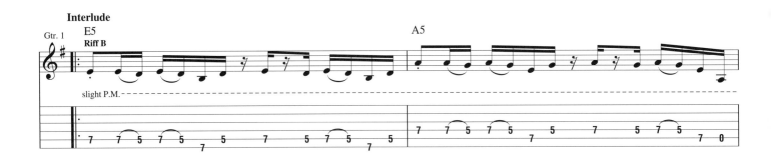

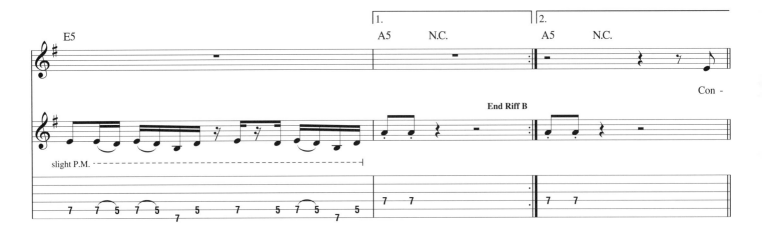

Con -

Outro

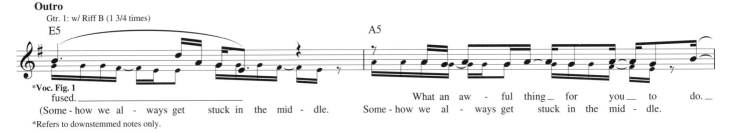

fused. _____

(Some - how we al - ways get stuck in the mid - dle.

What an aw - ful thing_ for you_ to do.

Some - how we al - ways get stuck in the mid - dle.

*Refers to downstemmed notes only.

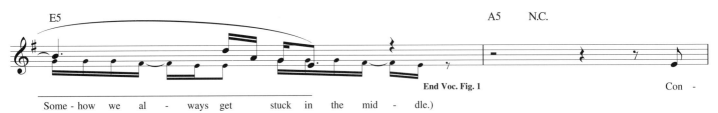

Some - how we al - ways get stuck in the mid - dle.)

Con -

fused. _____

What an aw - ful thing_ for you_ to say - ee.

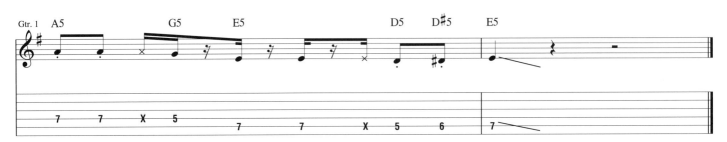

POSTERS

Words and Music by
Jack Johnson

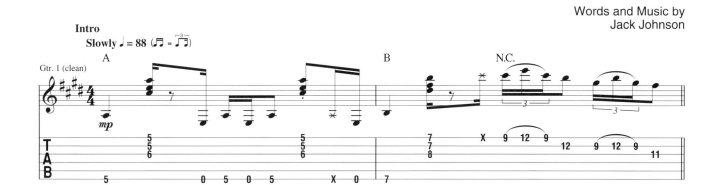

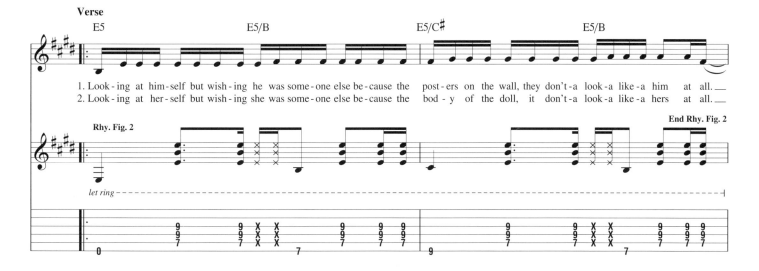

1. Look-ing at him-self but wish-ing he was some-one else be-cause the post-ers on the wall, they don't-a look-a like-a him at all. __
2. Look-ing at her-self but wish-ing she was some-one else be-cause the bod-y of the doll, it don't-a look-a like-a hers at all. __

So he ties it up, he tucks it in, he pulls it back and gives a grin,
So she straps it on, she sucks it in, she throws it up and gives a grin,

laugh-ing at him-self be-cause he knows he ain't loved at all._____
laugh-ing at her-self be-cause she knows she ain't that at all._____

He gets his
All

Chorus

cour-age from the can, it makes him feel like a man___ be-cause he's lov-ing all the la-dies, but the la-dies don't love him at all.
caught up in the trends, well, the truth be-gan to bend and the next thing you know, man, there just ain't no truth left at all.___

'Cause
'Cause when the

14

Gtr. 1: w/ Rhy. Fig. 3
Gtr. 2: w/ Riff A

when he's not drunk he's on-ly stuck on him-self, __ and then __ he has the nerve to say __ he needs a de-cent girl. __
pret-ty girl walks, she walks __ so proud, and when the pret-ty girl laughs, oh, man, __ she laughs __ so loud.

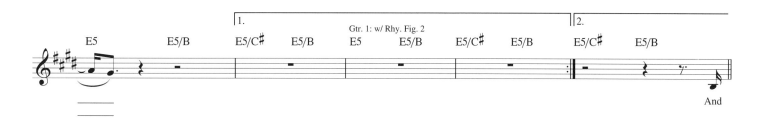

And

Bridge

if it ain't this, then it's that. As a mat-ter of fact, __ she has-n't had __ a day __ to re-lax

*Gtrs. 1 & 2

*Composite arrangement

since she __ lost her __ a-bil-i-ty __ to think __ clear-

Interlude

Gtr. 1: w/ Rhy. Fig. 1
Gtr. 2: w/ Riff A (last 2 meas)

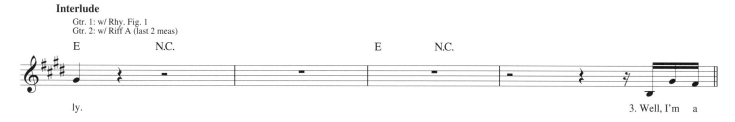

ly.

3. Well, I'm a

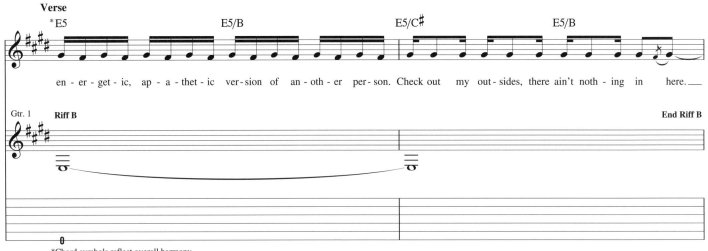

*Chord symbols reflect overall harmony.

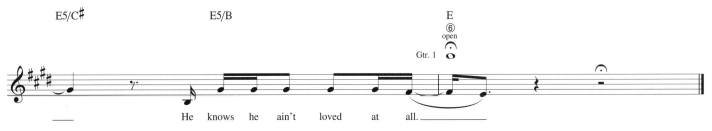

SEXY PLEXI

Words and Music by
Jack Johnson

18

FLAKE

Words and Music by
Jack Johnson

it pret-ty much al - ways means _____ "no." So don't _____

_____ tell _____ me _____ you might just let _____ it go. _____

End Rhy. Fig. 2

Gtrs. 1 & 2: w/ Rhy. Fig. 2

And of-ten-times we're la - zy, ___ it seems to stand in my ___ way. ___ 'Cause

no one, no, _____ not no _____ one likes to be let down. _____

Verse

Gtr. 2 tacet

Gtrs. 1 & 2

Gtr. 1

2. I know she loves the sun - rise, no long-er sees it with her sleep-ing eyes ___ and...

I know that when she said she's gon-na try, ___ well, it might not work be-cause of oth-er ties ___ and...

Gtr. 1: w/ Rhy. Fig. 1 (1 3/4 times)

3

I know she u - su - al - ly has some oth - er ties ___ and, ah, I would - n't want to break 'em, nah,

I would - n't want to break 'em. May - be she'll help me to un - tie ___ this, but

*Symbols in parentheses represent chord names respective to capoed guitar.
Symbols above reflect actual sounding chord. Capoed fret is "0" in tab.

Gtr. 3: w/ Riff A

It seems to me that "may - be," ___ it pret-ty much al - ways means ___ "no." So don't ___

___ tell ___ me ___ you might just let ___ it go. ___

Dobro Solo

Gtr. 3

Gtr. 4 (dobro)

w/ slide & pick

Gtr. 1

Gtrs. 1 & 4: w/ Rhy. Figs. 3 & 3A (6 times)

Gtr. 3

(The)

24

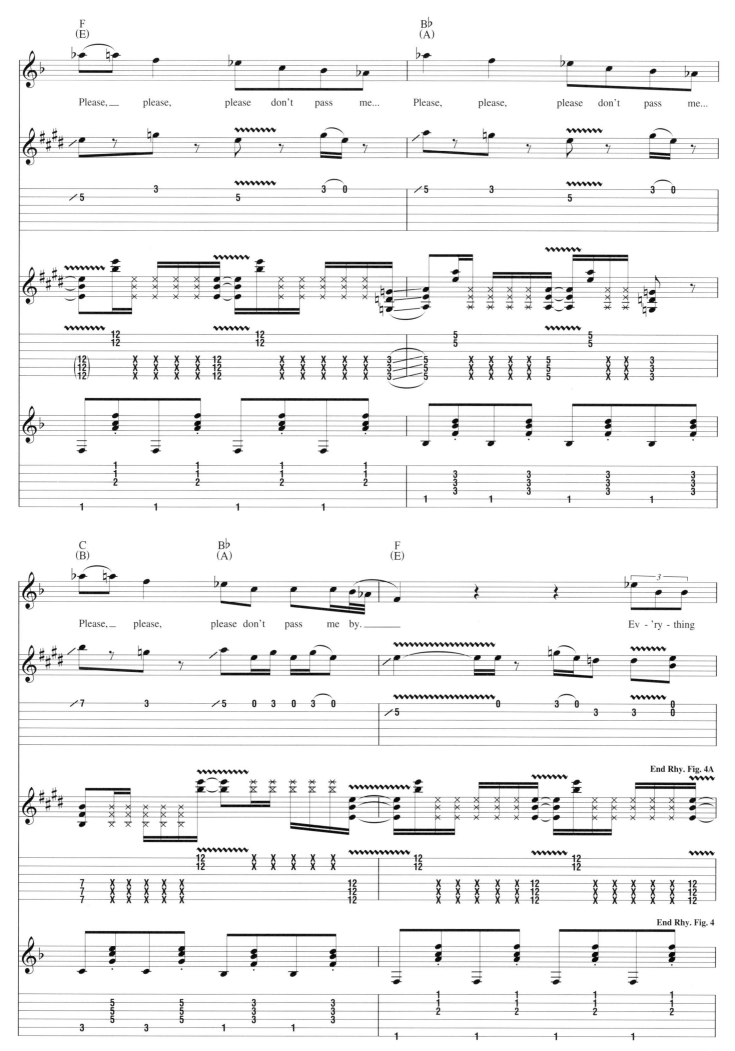

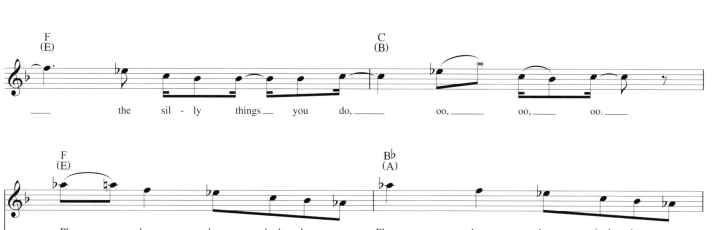

the sil - ly things____ you do,____ oo,____ oo,____ oo.____

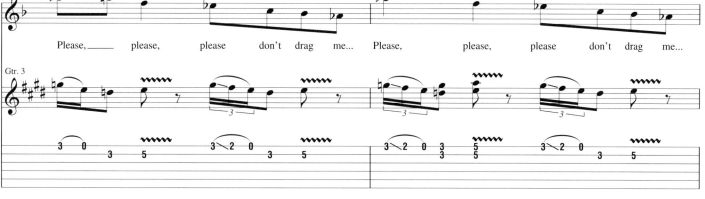

Please,____ please, please don't drag me... Please, please, please don't drag me...

Begin fade

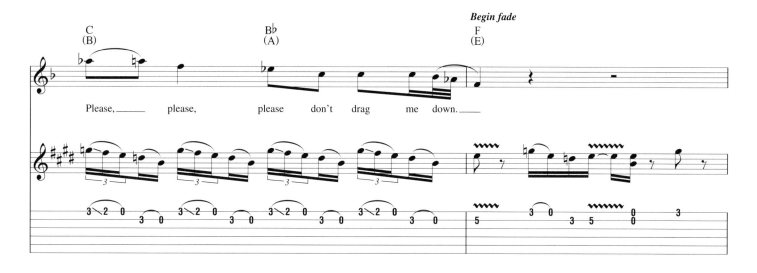

Please,____ please, please don't drag me down.____

Fade out

Gtr. 1 tacet
N.C.

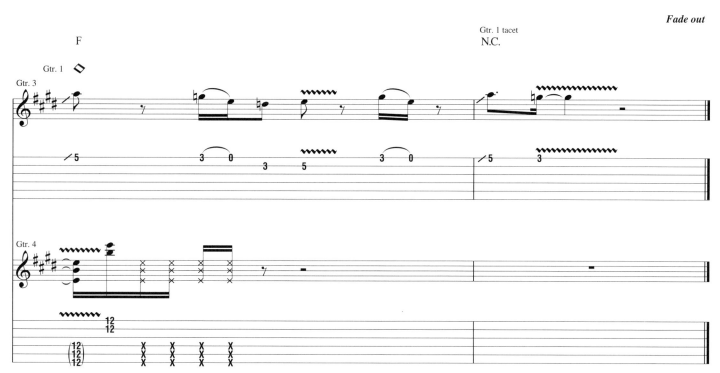

BUBBLE TOES

Words and Music by
Jack Johnson

30

Gtr. 1: w/ Rhy. Fig. 2

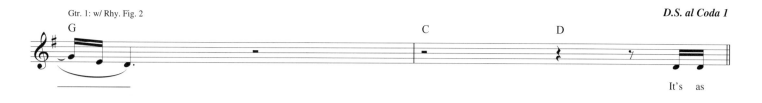

It's as

⊕ Coda 1

Gtr. 1 tacet

Bridge

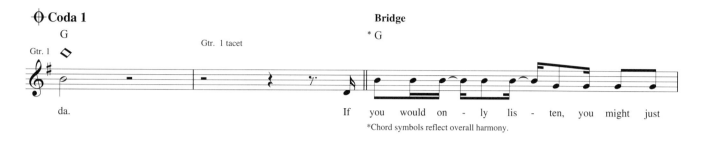

da.

If you would on - ly lis - ten, you might just

*Chord symbols reflect overall harmony.

real - ize what you're miss - ing, you're miss - ing me.

If you would on - ly lis - ten, you might just

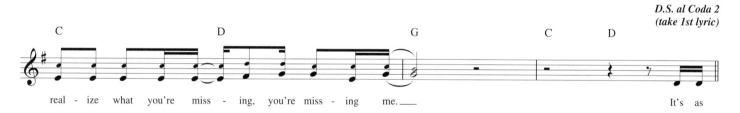

real - ize what you're miss - ing, you're miss - ing me. It's as

⊕ Coda 2

Gtr. 1: w/ Rhy. Fig. 2 (2 times)

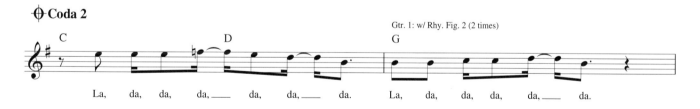

La, da, da, da, da, da, da. La, da, da, da, da, da.

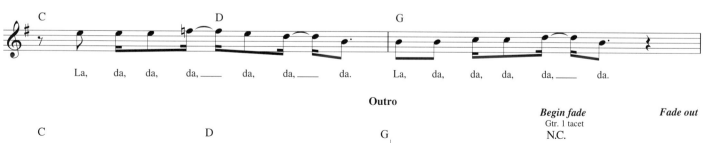

La, da, da, da, da, da, da. La, da, da, da, da, da.

Outro

Begin fade   *Fade out*

Gtr. 1 tacet

N.C.

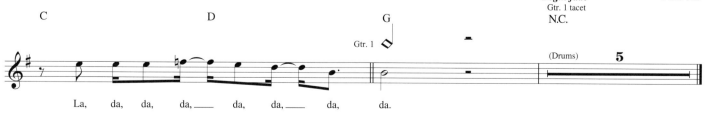

La, da, da, da, da, da, da, da.

31

FORTUNATE FOOL

Words and Music by
Jack Johnson

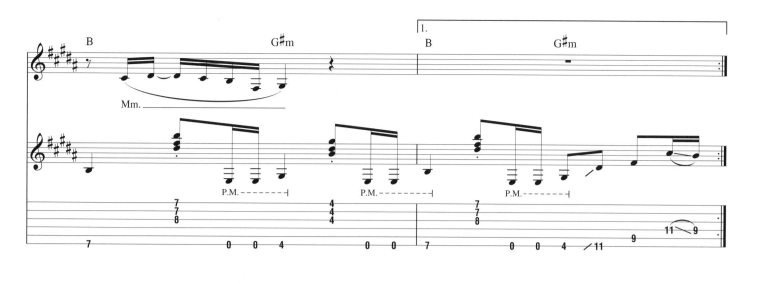

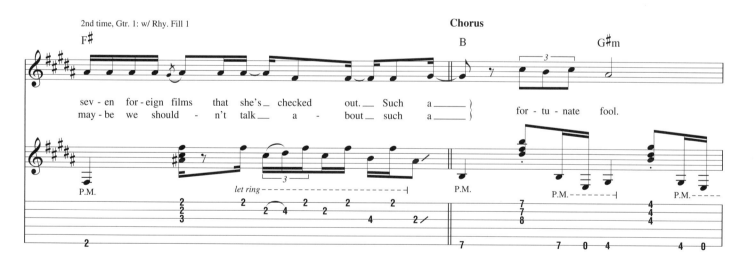

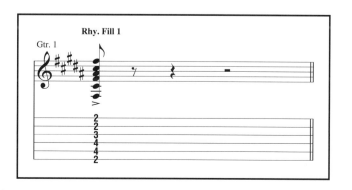

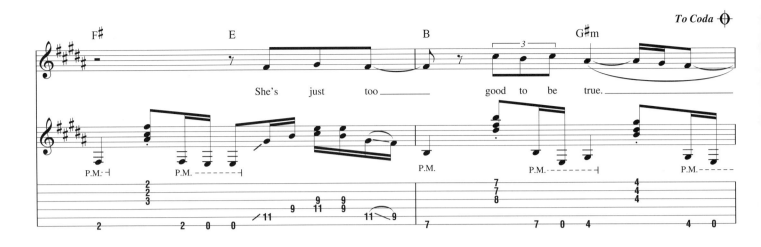

She's just too _____ good to be true.

She's such a _____ for-tu-nate fool.

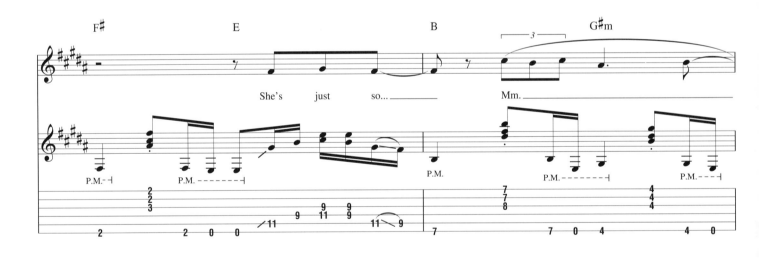

She's just so... _____ Mm. _____

Interlude

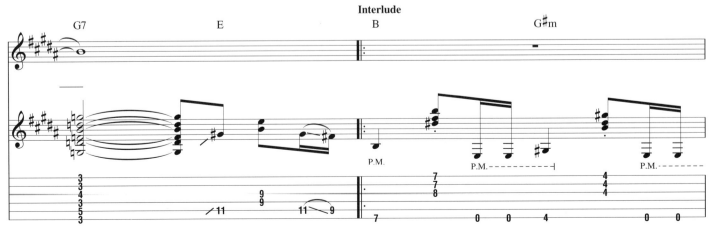

34

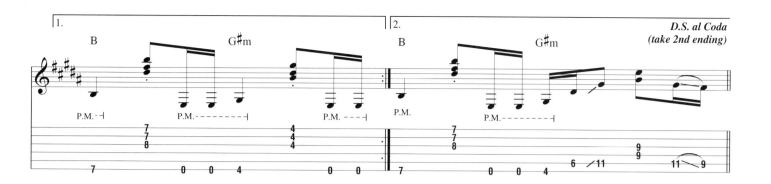

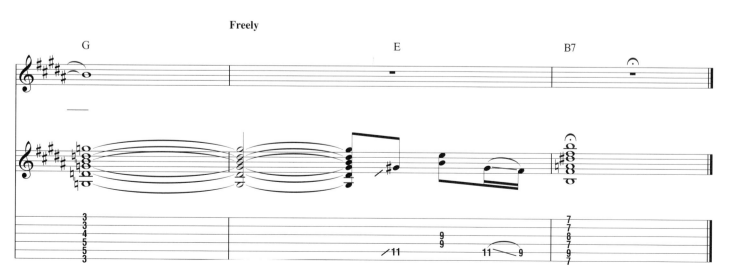

THE NEWS

Words and Music by
Jack Johnson

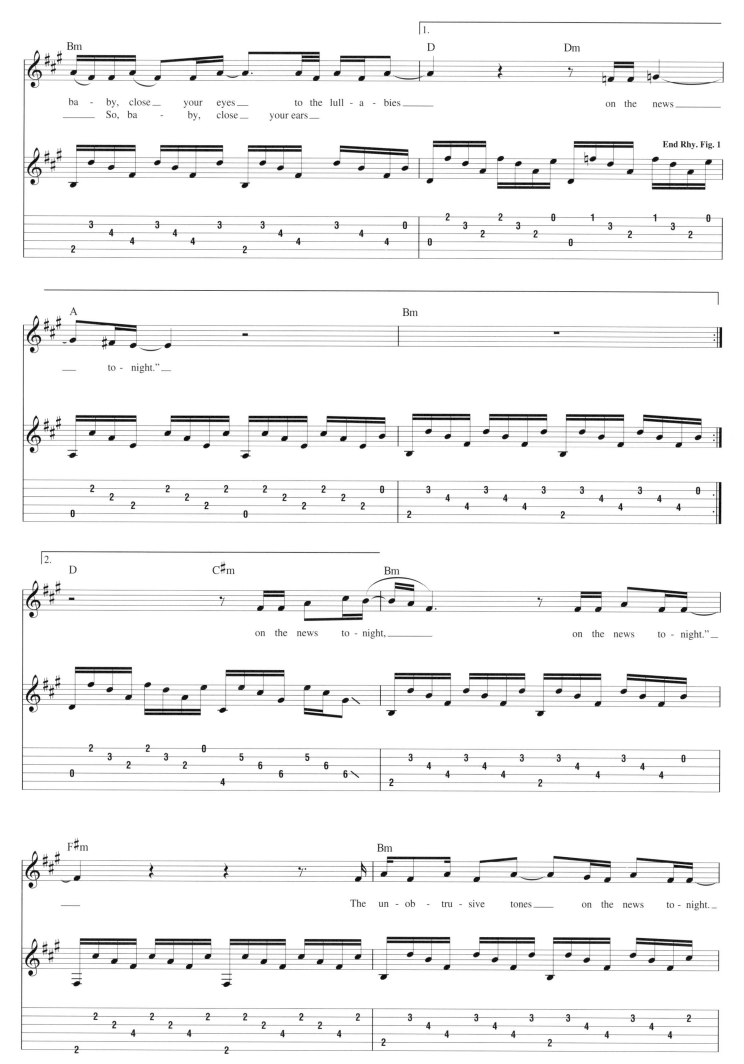

And Ma-ma said, "Mm."

Verse

Gtr. 1: w/ Rhy. Fig. 1

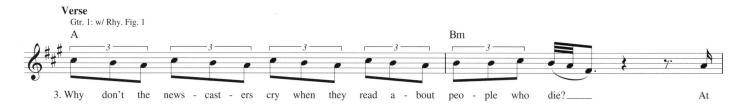

3. Why don't the news-cast-ers cry when they read a-bout peo-ple who die?___ At

least they could be de-cent e-nough to put just a tear in their eyes.___ Ma-ma said,___

___ "It's just make be-lieve,___ you can't be-lieve ev-'ry-thing you see.___ So,

ba - by, close___ your eyes___ to the lull-a-bies___ on the news___

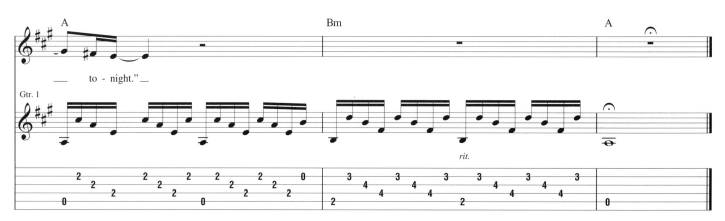

___ to - night."___

Gtr. 1

DRINK THE WATER

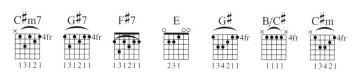

Words and Music by
Jack Johnson

Intro
Moderately ♩ = 96

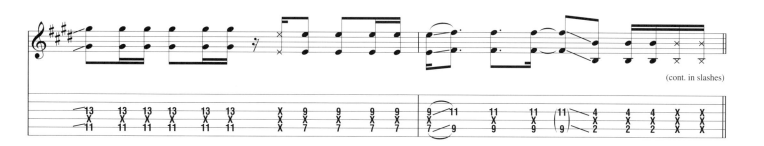

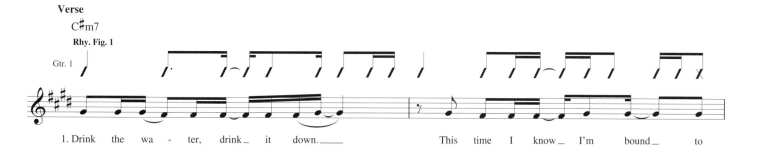

Verse

C#m7

Rhy. Fig. 1

Gtr. 1

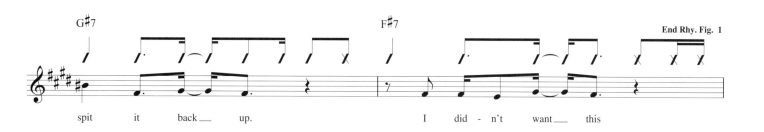

1. Drink the wa - ter, drink_ it down.____ This time I know_ I'm bound_ to

G#7   F#7   **End Rhy. Fig. 1**

spit   it   back____ up.   I   did - n't   want____ this

Gtr. 1: w/ Rhy. Fig. 1 (1 3/4 times)

C#m7

salt - y _____ sub - sti - tute,_____   just   not   a - go - in' to   do.____   I

need some _____ air _____ if I'm a - go - in' to live _____ through

this ex - pe - ri - ence. _____ Re - minds me of _____ a clock that

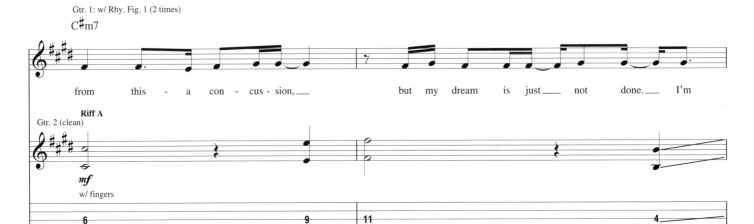

just won't _____ tick. _____ I want to wake _____ up

Gtr. 1: w/ Rhy. Fig. 1 (2 times)

from this - a con - cus - sion, _____ but my dream is just _____ not done. _____ I'm

Riff A
Gtr. 2 (clean)

mf

w/ fingers

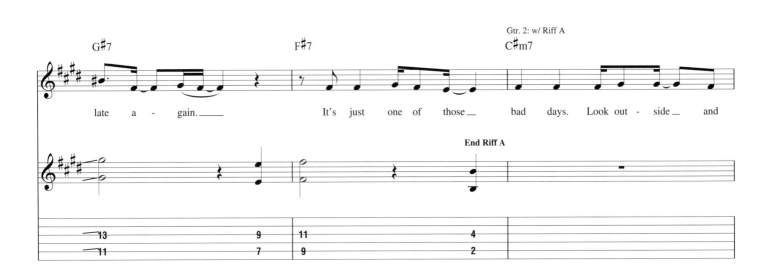

late a - gain. _____ It's just one of those _____ bad days. Look out - side _____ and

End Riff A

be care - ful what you ride. _____ You just might _____ find _____

*Composite arrangement

**Chords implied by bass.

43

MUDFOOTBALL
(FOR MOE LERNER)

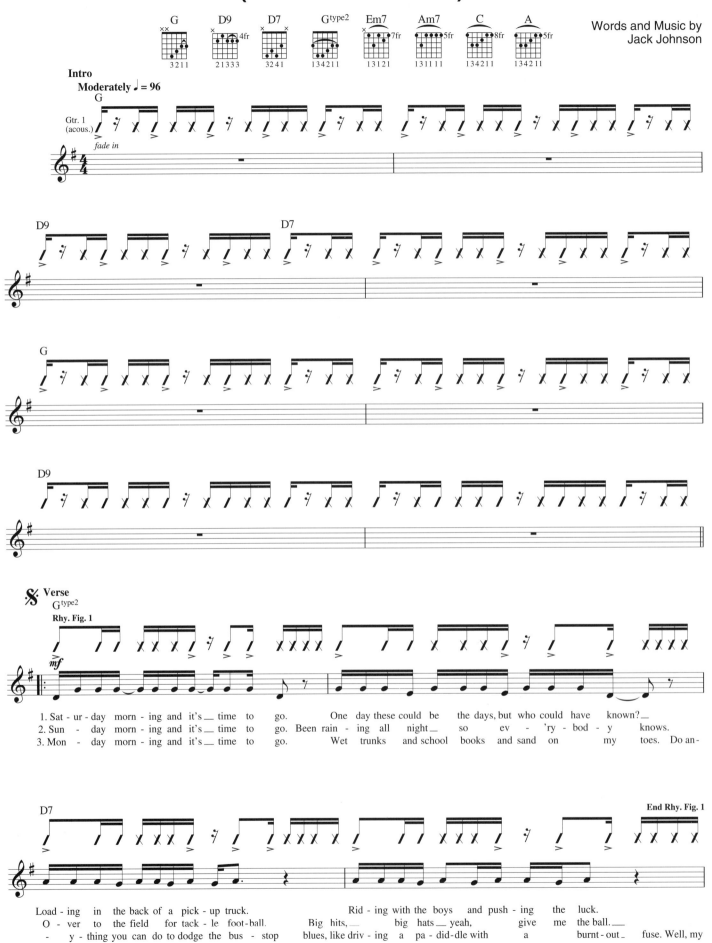

Words and Music by
Jack Johnson

1. Sat - ur - day morn - ing and it's __ time to go. One day these could be the days, but who could have known? __
2. Sun - day morn - ing and it's __ time to go. Been rain - ing all night __ so ev - 'ry - bod - y knows.
3. Mon - day morn - ing and it's __ time to go. Wet trunks and school books and sand on my toes. Do an-

Load - ing in the back of a pick - up truck. Rid - ing with the boys and push - ing the luck.
O - ver to the field for tack - le foot - ball. Big hits, __ big hats __ yeah, give me the ball. __
- y - thing you can do to dodge the bus - stop blues, like driv - ing a pa - did - dle with a burnt - out __ fuse. Well, my

Interlude

N.C.(G7)

Coda

Em7　Am7　C

We used___ to laugh___ a lot,___ but on - ly because___ we thought___ that ev -

A　C

-'ry - thing good al - ways would,___ ev - 'ry - thing good al - ways would___ re - main.

Gtype2　D7　Gtype2　D7

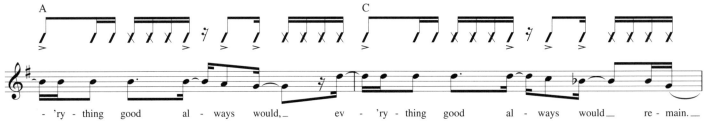

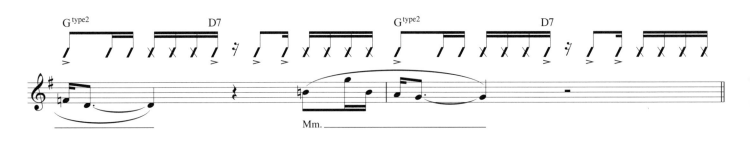

Mm._____

Outro

Gtr. 1: w/ Rhy. Fig. 2

Repeat and fade

G　D7

F-STOP BLUES

Words and Music by
Jack Johnson

1. Her-mit crabs and cow-ry shells__ crush be-neath his feet__ as he comes__ towards you. He's

wav-ing at you.__ Lift__ him

__ up to see what you can see.__ He be-gins his fo-cus-ing.__ He's

aim-ing at you.__ And now__ he has__

__ cut-a-ways from mem-o-ries,__ and __ close-ups__ of an-y-thing__ that

LOSING HOPE

Words and Music by
Jack Johnson

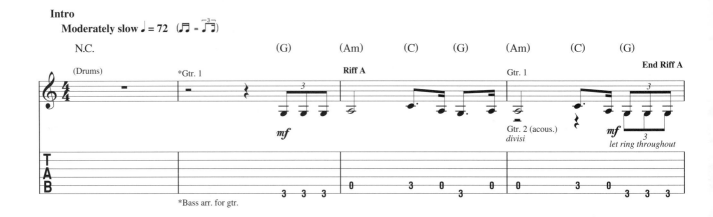

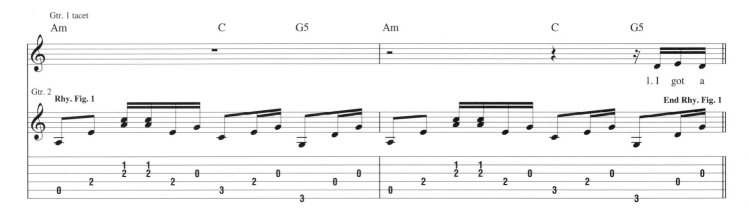

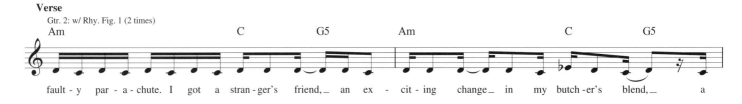

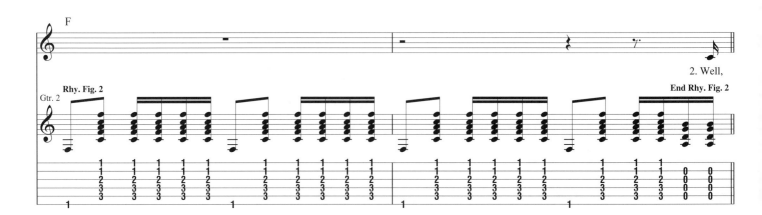

IT'S ALL UNDERSTOOD

Words and Music by
Jack Johnson

this part is good,_ and that's well_ un-der-stood,_ so you should laugh if you know what I mean._ But it's all_ rel-a-tive,_

Chorus

Gtr. 1: w/ Rhy. Fig. 1 (last meas.)
Gtr. 2 tacet

e-ven if you don't un-der-stand._ Well, it's all_ un-der-stood,_

Gtr. 1: w/ Rhy. Fig. 1

es-pe-cial'y when you don't un-der-stand._ Then it's all_ just be-cause_

Gtr. 1: w/ Rhy. Fig. 1 (last meas.)

e-ven if we don't un-der-stand,_ then let's all_ just_ be-lieve.

Gtr. 2 tacet

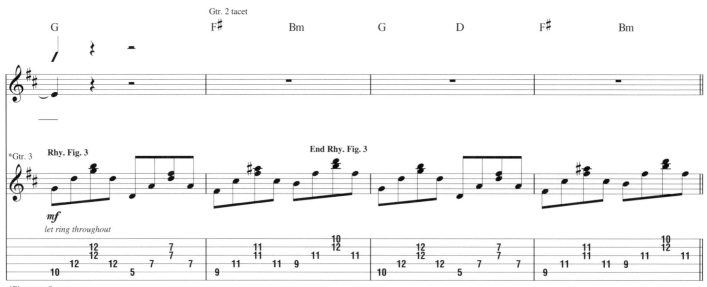

*Piano arr. for gtr.

Verse

Gtr. 3 tacet

2. Ev-'ry-one knows_ what went down_ be-cause the news was spread all o-ver town.___ And

*Piano arr. for gtr.

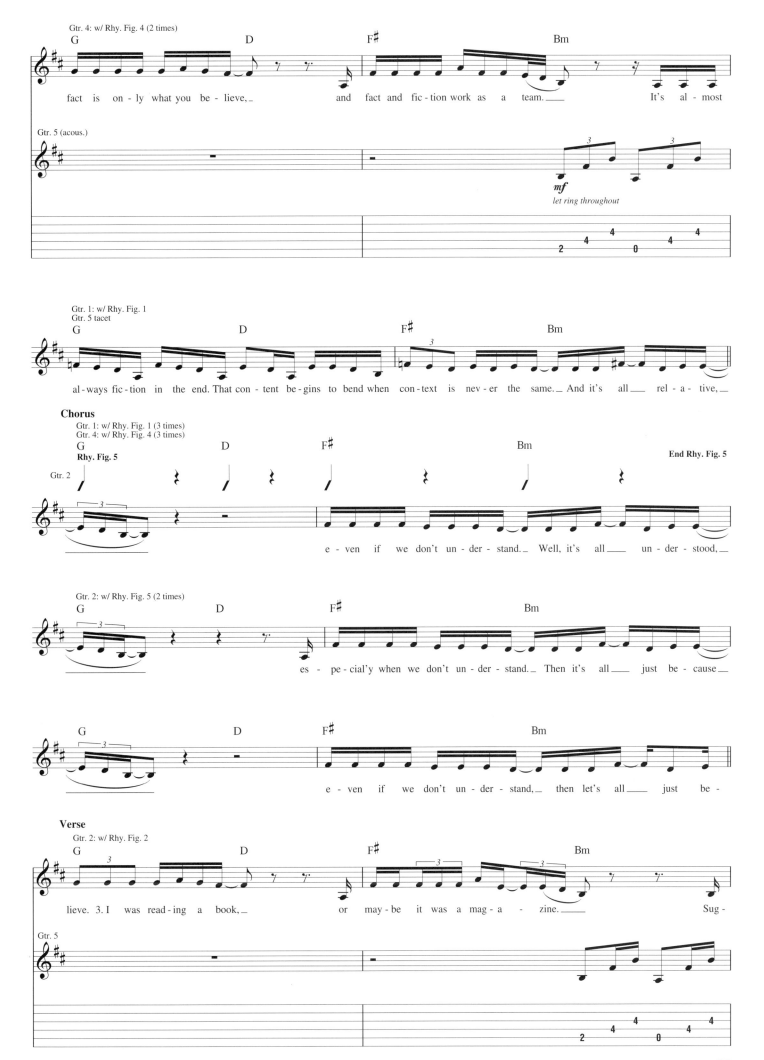

ges - tions on where to place faith. Sug - ges - tions on what to be - lieve. ___ But I

read some - where ___ that you've got ___ to be - ware. ___ You can't be - lieve an - y - thing ___ you read. ___ But the

good book is good ___ and that's well ___ un - der - stood, ___ so don't e - ven ques - tion if you know what I mean. ___ But it's all ___ rel - a - tive, ___

*Chords implied by bass.

Chorus

e - ven if you don't un - der - stand. ___ Well, it's all ___ un - der - stood, ___

**Backwards piano arr. for gtr.

es - pe - cial'y when you don't un - der - stand. ___ Then it's all ___ just be - cause ___

e - ven if we don't un - der - stand, ___ then let's all ___ just ___ be - lieve. ___

Outro

But there you go once a - gain. You

missed the point, and then you point your fin - gers at me ___

56

Guitar Notation Legend

Guitar Music can be notated three different ways: on a *musical staff*, in *tablature*, and in *rhythm slashes*.

RHYTHM SLASHES are written above the staff. Strum chords in the rhythm indicated. Use the chord diagrams found at the top of the first page of the transcription for the appropriate chord voicings. Round noteheads indicate single notes.

THE MUSICAL STAFF shows pitches and rhythms and is divided by bar lines into measures. Pitches are named after the first seven letters of the alphabet.

TABLATURE graphically represents the guitar fingerboard. Each horizontal line represents a a string, and each number represents a fret.

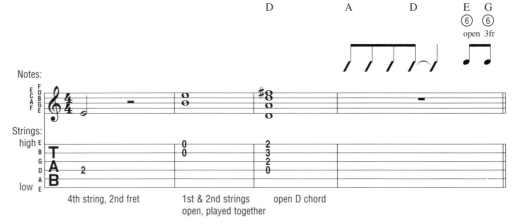

4th string, 2nd fret

1st & 2nd strings open, played together

open D chord

Definitions for Special Guitar Notation

HALF-STEP BEND: Strike the note and bend up 1/2 step.

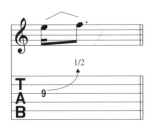

WHOLE-STEP BEND: Strike the note and bend up one step.

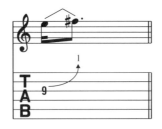

GRACE NOTE BEND: Strike the note and immediately bend up as indicated.

SLIGHT (MICROTONE) BEND: Strike the note and bend up 1/4 step.

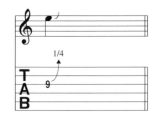

BEND AND RELEASE: Strike the note and bend up as indicated, then release back to the original note. Only the first note is struck.

PRE-BEND: Bend the note as indicated, then strike it.

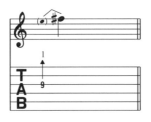

PRE-BEND AND RELEASE: Bend the note as indicated. Strike it and release the bend back to the original note.

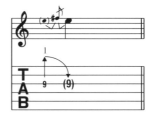

UNISON BEND: Strike the two notes simultaneously and bend the lower note up to the pitch of the higher.

VIBRATO: The string is vibrated by rapidly bending and releasing the note with the fretting hand.

WIDE VIBRATO: The pitch is varied to a greater degree by vibrating with the fretting hand.

HAMMER-ON: Strike the first (lower) note with one finger, then sound the higher note (on the same string) with another finger by fretting it without picking.

PULL-OFF: Place both fingers on the notes to be sounded. Strike the first note and without picking, pull the finger off to sound the second (lower) note.

LEGATO SLIDE: Strike the first note and then slide the same fret-hand finger up or down to the second note. The second note is not struck.

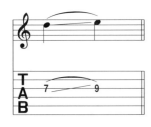

SHIFT SLIDE: Same as legato slide, except the second note is struck.

TRILL: Very rapidly alternate between the notes indicated by continuously hammering on and pulling off.

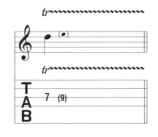

TAPPING: Hammer ("tap") the fret indicated with the pick-hand index or middle finger and pull off to the note fretted by the fret hand.

NATURAL HARMONIC: Strike the note while the fret-hand lightly touches the string directly over the fret indicated.

PINCH HARMONIC: The note is fretted normally and a harmonic is produced by adding the edge of the thumb or the tip of the index finger of the pick hand to the normal pick attack.

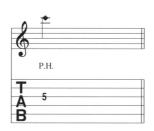

HARP HARMONIC: The note is fretted normally and a harmonic is produced by gently resting the pick hand's index finger directly above the indicated fret (in parentheses) while the pick hand's thumb or pick assists by plucking the appropriate string.

PICK SCRAPE: The edge of the pick is rubbed down (or up) the string, producing a scratchy sound.

MUFFLED STRINGS: A percussive sound is produced by laying the fret hand across the string(s) without depressing, and striking them with the pick hand.

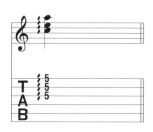

PALM MUTING: The note is partially muted by the pick hand lightly touching the string(s) just before the bridge.

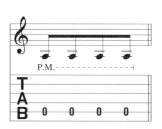

RAKE: Drag the pick across the strings indicated with a single motion.

TREMOLO PICKING: The note is picked as rapidly and continuously as possible.

ARPEGGIATE: Play the notes of the chord indicated by quickly rolling them from bottom to top.

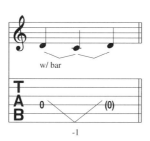

VIBRATO BAR DIVE AND RETURN: The pitch of the note or chord is dropped a specified number of steps (in rhythm) then returned to the original pitch.

VIBRATO BAR SCOOP: Depress the bar just before striking the note, then quickly release the bar.

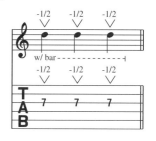

VIBRATO BAR DIP: Strike the note and then immediately drop a specified number of steps, then release back to the original pitch.

Additional Musical Definitions

 (accent)
- Accentuate note (play it louder)

 (accent)
- Accentuate note with great intensity

 (staccato)
- Play the note short

- Downstroke

∨
- Upstroke

D.S. al Coda
- Go back to the sign (𝄋), then play until the measure marked "***To Coda***," then skip to the section labelled "**Coda**."

D.C. al Fine
- Go back to the beginning of the song and play until the measure marked "***Fine***" (end).

Rhy. Fig.
- Label used to recall a recurring accompaniment pattern (usually chordal).

Riff
- Label used to recall composed, melodic lines (usually single notes) which recur.

Fill
- Label used to identify a brief melodic figure which is to be inserted into the arrangement.

Rhy. Fill
- A chordal version of a Fill.

tacet
- Instrument is silent (drops out).

- Repeat measures between signs.

- When a repeated section has different endings, play the first ending only the first time and the second ending only the second time.

NOTE: Tablature numbers in parentheses mean:
1. The note is being sustained over a system (note in standard notation is tied), or
2. The note is sustained, but a new articulation (such as a hammer-on, pull-off, slide or vibrato begins), or
3. The note is a barely audible "ghost" note (note in standard notation is also in parentheses).

CHERRY LANE MUSIC COMPANY

6 East 32nd Street, New York, NY 10016

Quality in Printed Music

Guitar ™

The Magazine You Can Play

Visit the Guitar One web site at **www.guitarone.com**

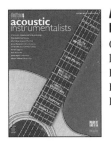

ACOUSTIC INSTRUMENTALISTS
INCLUDES TAB

Over 15 transcriptions from legendary artists such as Leo Kottke, John Fahey, Jorma Kaukonen, Chet Atkins, Adrian Legg, Jeff Beck, and more.

02500399 Play-It-Like-It-Is Guitar............$9.95

THE BEST BASS LINES

24 super songs: Bohemian Rhapsody • Celebrity Skin • Crash Into Me • Crazy Train • Glycerine • Money • November Rain • Smoke on the Water • Sweet Child O' Mine • What Would You Say • You're My Flavor • and more.
02500311 Play-It-Like-It-Is Bass $14.95

BLUES TAB
INCLUDES TAB

14 songs: Boom Boom • Cold Shot • Hide Away • I Can't Quit You Baby • I'm Your Hoochie Coochie Man • In 2 Deep • It Hurts Me Too • Talk to Your Daughter • The Thrill Is Gone • and more.
02500410 Play-It-Like-It-Is Guitar............$14.95

CLASSIC ROCK TAB
INCLUDES TAB

15 rock hits: Cat Scratch Fever • Crazy Train • Day Tripper • Hey Joe • Hot Blooded • Start Me Up • We Will Rock You • You Really Got Me • and more.
02500408 Play-It-Like-It-Is Guitar............$14.95

MODERN ROCK TAB
INCLUDES TAB

15 of modern rock's best: Are You Gonna Go My Way • Denial • Hanging by a Moment • I Did It • My Hero • Nobody's Real • Rock the Party (Off the Hook) • Shock the Monkey • Slide • Spit It Out • and more.
02500409 Play-It-Like-It-Is Guitar............$14.95

SIGNATURE SONGS
INCLUDES TAB

21 artists' trademark hits: Crazy Train (Ozzy Osbourne) • My Generation (The Who) • Smooth (Santana) • Sunshine of Your Love (Cream) • Walk This Way (Aerosmith) • Welcome to the Jungle (Guns N' Roses) • What Would You Say (Dave Matthews Band) • and more.
02500303 Play-It-Like-It-Is Guitar............$16.95

BASS SECRETS

WHERE TODAY'S BASS STYLISTS GET TO THE BOTTOM LINE
compiled by John Stix
Bass Secrets brings together 48 columns highlighting specific topics – ranging from the technical to the philosophical – from masters such as Stu Hamm, Randy Coven, Tony Franklin and Billy Sheehan. They cover topics including tapping, walking bass lines, soloing, hand positions, harmonics and more. Clearly illustrated with musical examples.
02500100 ....$12.95

CLASSICS ILLUSTRATED

WHERE BACH MEETS ROCK
by Robert Phillips
Classics Illustrated is designed to demonstrate for readers and players the links between rock and classical music. Each of the 30 columns from *Guitar* highlights one musical concept and provides clear examples in both styles of music. This cool book lets you study moving bass lines over stationary chords in the music of Bach and Guns N' Roses, learn the similarities between "Leyenda" and "Diary of a Madman," and much more!
02500101 ....$9.95

GUITAR SECRETS
INCLUDES TAB

WHERE ROCK'S GUITAR MASTERS SHARE THEIR TRICKS, TIPS & TECHNIQUES
compiled by John Stix
This unique and informative compilation features 42 columns culled from *Guitar* magazine. Readers will discover dozens of techniques and playing tips, and gain practical advice and words of wisdom from guitar masters.
02500099 ....$10.95

IN THE LISTENING ROOM

WHERE ARTISTS CRITIQUE THE MUSIC OF THEIR PEERS
compiled by John Stix
A compilation of 75 columns from *Guitar* magazine, *In the Listening Room* provides a unique opportunity for readers to hear major recording artists remark on the music of their peers. These artists were given no information about what they would hear, and their comments often tell as much about themselves as they do about the music they listened to. Includes candid critiques by music legends like Aerosmith, Jeff Beck, Jack Bruce, Dimebag Darrell, Buddy Guy, Kirk Hammett, Eric Johnson, John McLaughlin, Dave Navarro, Carlos Santana, Joe Satriani, Stevie Ray Vaughan, and many others.
02500097 ....$14.95

Visit Cherry Lane online at **www.cherrylane.com**

LEGENDS OF LEAD GUITAR

THE BEST OF INTERVIEWS: 1995-2000
This is a fascinating compilation of interviews with today's greatest guitarists! From deeply rooted blues giants to the most fearless pioneers, legendary players reveal how they achieve their extraordinary craft.
02500329 ....$14.95

LESSON LAB

This exceptional book/CD pack features more than 20 in-depth lessons. Tackle in detail a variety of pertinent music- and guitar-related subjects, such as scales, chords, theory, guitar technique, songwriting, and much more!
02500330 Book/CD Pack......................$19.95

NOISE & FEEDBACK

THE BEST OF 1995-2000: YOUR QUESTIONS ANSWERED
If you ever wanted to know about a specific guitar lick, trick, technique or effect, this book/CD pack is for you! It features over 70 lessons on composing • computer assistance • education and career advice • equipment • technique • terminology and notation • tunings • and more.
02500328 Book/CD Pack......................$17.95

OPEN EARS

A JOURNEY THROUGH LIFE WITH GUITAR IN HAND
by Steve Morse
In this collection of 50 *Guitar* magazine columns from the mid-'90s on, guitarist Steve Morse sets the story straight about what being a working musician *really* means. He deals out practical advice on: playing with the band, songwriting, recording and equipment, and more, through anecdotes of his hard-knock lessons learned.
02500333 ....$10.95

SPOTLIGHT ON STYLE

THE BEST OF 1995-2000: AN EXPLORER'S GUIDE TO GUITAR
This book and CD cover 18 of the world's most popular guitar styles, including: blues guitar • classical guitar • country guitar • funk guitar • jazz guitar • Latin guitar • metal • rockabilly and more!
02500320 Book/CD Pack......................$19.95

STUDIO CITY

PROFESSIONAL SESSION RECORDING FOR GUITARISTS
by Carl Verheyen
In this collection of colomns from Guitar Magazine, guitarists will learn how to: exercise studio etiquette and act professionally • acquire, assemble and set up gear for sessions • use the tricks of the trade to become a studio hero • get repeat call-backs • and more.
02500195 ....$9.95

GREAT STEELY DAN BOOKS

from CHERRY LANE MUSIC COMPANY

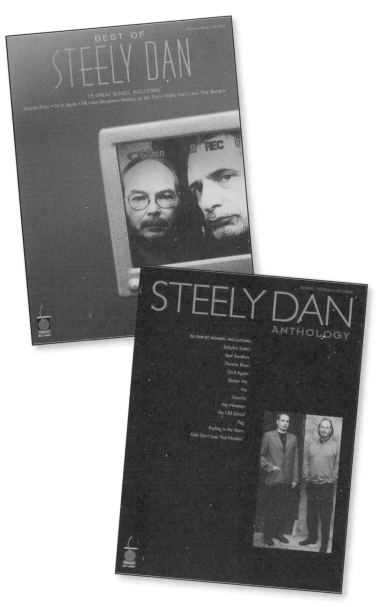

STEELY DAN'S GREATEST SONGS
15 more trademark Steely Dan songs, including: Aja • Chain Lightning • Daddy Don't Live in That New York City No More • Everyone's Gone to the Movies • Haitian Divorce • Josie • Pretzel Logic • Reeling in the Years • and more.
02500168 Play-It-Like-It-Is Guitar $19.95

BEST OF STEELY DAN FOR SOLO GUITAR
11 great solos, including: Aja • Babylon Sisters • Deacon Blues • Doctor Wu • Gaucho • Haitian Divorce • Hey Nineteen • Kid Charlemagne • Peg • Rikki Don't Lose That Number • Third World Man.
02500169 Solo Guitar...$12.95

BEST OF STEELY DAN FOR DRUMS
10 classic songs for drums from Steely Dan. Includes: Aja • Babylon Sisters • The Fez • Peg • Two Against Nature • Time Out of Mind • What a Shame About Me • and more.
02500312 Drums $18.95

STEELY DAN LEGENDARY LICKS (GUITAR)
28 extensive musical examples from: Aja • Babylon Sisters • Black Cow • Bodhisattva • Josie • Kid Charlemagne • Parker's Band • Peg • Reeling in the Years • Rikki Don't Lose That Number • and many more.
02500160 Guitar Book/CD Pack...$19.95

STEELY DAN JUST THE RIFFS FOR GUITAR
by Rich Zurkowski
More than 40 hot licks from Steely Dan. Includes: Babylon Sisters • Black Friday • The Boston Rag • Deacon Blues • Kid Charlemagne • King of the World • Peg • Reeling in the Years • Rikki Don't Lose That Number • Sign in Stranger • and more.
02500159 Just the Riffs – Guitar...$19.95

THE ART OF STEELY DAN (KEYBOARD)
Features over 30 great Steely Dan tunes for piano: Aja • Black Cow • Bodhisattva • Hey Nineteen • I.G.Y. (What a Beautiful World) • Parker's Band • Reeling in the Years • Third World Man • Your Gold Teeth II • many more.
02500171 Piano Solo $19.95

STEELY DAN JUST THE RIFFS FOR KEYBOARD
28 keyboard riffs, including: Babylon Sisters • The Boston Rag • Deacon Blues • Don't Take Me Alive • Green Earrings • Hey Nineteen • Peg • Reeling in the Years • Rikki Don't Lose That Number • and more.
02500164 Just the Riffs – Keyboard $9.95

Prices, contents, and availability subject to change without notice.

BEST OF STEELY DAN
A fantastic collection of 15 hits showcasing the sophistocated sounds of Steely Dan. Includes: Babylon Sisters • Bad Sneakers • Deacon Blues • Do It Again • FM • Here at the Western World • Hey Nineteen • I.G.Y. (What a Beautiful World) • Josie • Kid Charlemagne • My Old School • Peg • Reeling in the Years • Rikki Don't Lose That Number • Time out of Mind.
02500165 Piano/Vocal/Guitar..$14.95

STEELY DAN – ANTHOLOGY
A comprehensive collection of 30 of their biggest hits, including: Aja • Big Noise, New York • Black Cow • Black Friday • Bodhisattva • Deacon Blues • Do It Again • Everyone's Gone to the Movies • FM • Gaucho • Hey Nineteen • Josie • Reeling in the Years • more!
02500166 Piano/Vocal/Guitar..$17.95

BEST OF STEELY DAN FOR GUITAR
15 transcriptions of Steely Dan's jazz/rock tunes, including: Bad Sneakers • Black Friday • The Boston Rag • Deacon Blues • FM • Green Earrings • Kid Charlemagne • Parker's Band • Peg • Rikki Don't Lose That Number • Third World Man • Time Out of Mind • and more.
02500167 Play-It-Like-It-Is Guitar $19.95

CHERRY LANE MUSIC COMPANY
6 East 32nd Street, New York, NY 10016

EXCLUSIVELY DISTRIBUTED BY

HAL•LEONARD® CORPORATION
7777 W. BLUEMOUND RD. P.O. BOX 13819 MILWAUKEE, WI 53213

http://www.halleonard.com

0401

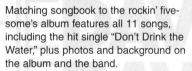